孟煌 MENG HUANG

我和我们 I AND WE

本画册为孟煌个展 "我和我们" 而出版
2012年1月27日至3月31日展出于瑞士卢森麦勒画廊 北京-卢森

This catalogue was published on the occasion of Meng Huang's solo exhibition "I and We"
at Galerie Urs Meile, Beijing-Lucerne, Lucerne, Switzerland, from January 27 to March 31, 2012

致谢

Elisabeth Brinkmeier, Monica Dematté, 贾枝平, 孟辉, Florian Richter, Timm Walker, 王少波, 王勇波, 张伟,
以及麦勒画廊 北京-卢森 全体工作人员。

Acknowledgements

Elisabeth Brinkmeier, Monica Dematté, Jia Zhiping, Meng Hui, Florian Richter, Timm Walker, Wang Shaobo, Wang Yongbo,
Zhang Wei, and the staff at Galerie Urs Meile, Beijing-Lucerne.

目录
CONTENTS

渐隐的本源
—— 有关孟煌创作的若干思考

文：Heinz-Norbert Jocks

孟煌1966年生于北京，他不是安迪·沃霍尔那种极度热衷于不断一再创造自我的艺术家，却也无法在自己所做的任何事情中完全忘掉自己。因此我们可以认为，这位以绘画为主，兼做摄影的艺术家，他的作品都间接或直接地指向了他的生活和生存状态。是的，从根本上来讲，有关自身思考和观看的问题对他来说是无法回避的，这也是他与世界发生摩擦、不断地创作下一个作品的原因。

我们可以从他1993年至2002年间创作的系列绘画《失乐园》开始讨论。我们看到的是街景、建筑、厂房、街灯、旷野中零星的树；荒凉、甚至令人不安的风景，还有天空和云朵。没有什么是温馨或诱人的，也没有什么严格意义上的美或者崇高的东西，只有跟沉没于黑夜之中的外部世界的纯然对峙，在与一种覆盖一切的空无对应着，而画中的外部空间虽然也有一些人类的痕迹，却被无可消溶的陌生感紧紧笼罩着，孟煌的目光是"地球上最后一人"的目光。是的，我们甚至可以说，活生生的能够侵入肌肤、横扫一切的孤独感，正在通过画布上的每个细孔击中我们、进入我们。

那些风景并没有什么特指，孟煌在与萧岭（Nataline Colonnello）的一次颇有启发性的对话中如此表述。那时，他白天睡觉，晚上工作，醒来时，黑夜已然降临，世界对他来说充满了不真实，只有事物的影子在纠缠着他。与白天隔绝，冷漠世界的巨大阴影投射在徘徊于外的灵魂之上，没有光，没有色彩；在那些黑暗、可怕的画面中，一切存在之物不可探知、无法理喻的特质变得可感可知。乐园远不可及，在孟煌眼中，它却是一场美妙而无法实现的白日梦，他也无法想象某种黄金时代，想象那种万物一体、琴瑟和谐的景象。那么，他的画被如此极度绝望的基调充斥，无法抑制的失落感在那里向我们倾诉，便绝非偶然。孩童时代的他就已觉晓自己身处于一个满是忧郁、毫无指望的世界。乐园早已失落，从来没有过幸福的秘密花园，有的只是对无所归属的痛楚，永不消亡。

画面投向幽深渊远之处的失望的目光，也反映了一位艺术家存在主义的极端主观性，他时刻想要超越"虚假"竖立起来的高高的围墙。我们清楚地听到：去生活，去创作，去对抗那种想要吞噬一切的超强大的随波逐流。多数人追求的群体归属感所能带来的惬意，显然不在这位顽固的艺术家个人的愿望清单上，他无法摆脱个人对世界的不满。这可能也是为什么他会坚定地站在那些拒绝诱惑、胁迫和拒绝同化的人的一边。

是的，对于这位为"真"而苦苦纠缠的艺术家来说，成为某种东西的一部分是令人怀疑的。他只能保持距离，他宁可在门槛上徘徊，就像1993年底穿越中国西北那样。那时，火车开在戈壁滩上，是如此之慢，车里的人几乎感觉不到列车的移动，一种动中之静。孟煌站在两节车厢的过道处，他往前看，向后瞧，他望出窗外。一种中间地带的生存，一种家不在这里也不在那里、始终被关在外面所以在一切之外的感觉。然后突然，远处废旧工厂的烟囱吐出一道烟，于他至关重要的一秒钟，他被这个景致真

The Gradual Disappearance of the Source
A Few Thoughts on the Works of Meng Huang

by Heinz-Norbert Jocks

As an artist, Meng Huang (* in Beijing in 1966) does not play the role of auto-fictionist, one who loves reinventing himself constantly, as Andy Warhol did. Nor is he completely able to disregard himself in everything that he undertakes. In this respect, everything that he produces as both a painter and a photographer contains direct as well as indirect references to his life, his existence. Yes, fundamentally speaking, the inevitable process of questioning his own ideas and perceptions is the inexhaustible source behind his artistic friction with the world, continually compelling him to create more works of art.

Let us take his cycle of paintings, *Paradise Lost* (1993–2002), as a starting point: we see views of streets. Houses. Industrial buildings. Street lamps. Broad fields with lone trees. Actually inhospitable, even alienating landscapes. Added to that: sky and clouds. Nothing cozy and inviting. Also nothing beautiful or even sublime, in the narrow sense of the word. Instead, the pure confrontation with an exterior immersed in the dark of night, corresponding with the emptiness that blankets everything. These exteriors, in which we also encounter signs of human presence, attest to the vast density of indissoluble alienation. All in all, the gaze that Meng Huang turns upon it seems like the gaze of one of the last men on earth. Yes, one might say, the wholly assertive atmosphere of loneliness, which gets under the skin, penetrates through all of the pores of his painting, moving directly toward us and into us.

This does not refer to anything in specific, as Meng Huang once said in an informative conversation with Nataline Colonnello. At the time he was making those paintings, he was sleeping during the day and awake and working at night. Since the world was already dark when he woke up, it seemed fully unreal to him, because only the shadows of things stood out. A sense of being outdoors, separated from daytime, in the extreme chill of a world without light and colors, is as tangibly present in the gloomy, eerie paintings as is the immensity and incomprehensibility of all that exists. As distant and unattainable as the paradise here seems to be—for it is, after all, in the eyes of Meng Huang, a beautiful but ultimately unrealizable daydream—it is just as difficult for him to imagine a golden age, when everything was still harmoniously at peace with everything else. It is no accident that these paintings are marked by an atmosphere of extreme despondency; they seem to speak to us out of a sense of insurmountable forlornness. Even as a child, he felt that he was at the mercy of a world full of sadness, where there was no way out, and paradise was eternally lost. No secret garden of happiness, but an ineluctable suffering caused by a sense of not belonging.

The disappointed perspective of depth and mystery that emanates from these paintings also mirrors the existential ultra-subjectivity of an artist who is constantly trying to surmount the high walls of inauthenticity. Obviously, these paintings resound with the sense of fragility in life and work that comes from resisting the superpower of conformity that tries to engulf everything. That feeling of well-being that stems from belonging to a group or collective, which most people long for, is surely not on the wish list of a resistant artist who cannot rid himself—or so it seems to him—of his personal discomfort with the world. This is probably also why he so clearly takes the side of those who resist the seduction or compulsion to adapt, those who make a stand.

Yes, to this artist, who wrestles for the truth, who does not want to be swallowed up, being part of something seems rather suspect. He cannot help but keep his distance, and prefers to linger on the threshold. For instance, there was the time, in late 1993, when he traveled northwest through China. At the time, the train crossed the desert at such a slow, creeping pace that the travelers felt as if they were hardly moving at all. At a standstill, in motion. He would stand in the space between the cars, where he could see ahead of him, behind him, and out the windows. A life in transition, neither here, nor completely at home there, but always excluded, with a sense of being outside of it all. In the distance, suddenly the smokestack of a demolished

的感动了，心仿佛被陨石击中，不，更加强烈，他有了肌肤之痛，好像心被针刺穿。从此，烟囱对于孟煌，便成了绝望的一个一个灵魂的象征，不断出现在他的创作之中。

不光鉴于这样的一个视觉世界，也就孟煌其他色彩缺席的风景作品而言，那幅描绘一只被捏皱了的香烟盒的作品《烟盒》（2011，布面油画，335 x 420 cm: 5x 335 x 84 cm）粗看不觉会让人诧异、疑惑。显然，孟煌赋予了这个图像相当重要的意义，因为他不仅用了大尺寸来表现它，还让它跟另外20幅小画组成一个系列（《香烟 No.1》-《香烟 No.20》2011，布面油画，各80 x 80 cm）。我们看到，黑色烟灰缸里摁灭的烟头，第一幅中只有一个烟头，然后是两个、三个，直至二十个，"烟头画"的数量正好跟一盒烟里烟的数量相同。为什么？一个来自西方的人或许会不由自主地迅速作出比较，并问：这位艺术家为什么现在突然对平凡琐碎之物的审美有了兴趣？他背叛自己的艺术原则了吗？他从现在起只关心所谓的幸福和忘却自我时的轻松愉悦了吗？还是他于浮光掠影中不经意地滑向了波普艺术的航道？他了解法国新现实主义的作品吗？或许他只在关注包装品的商业美学？然而，此类艺术史性质的猜测无助于我们，反而会诱使我们偏离关键所在，走上迷津，无法探究表面背后的文章。孟煌无意引述艺术史。那些他亲身经历过的、逼迫他、压制他、并在威胁着个体生命的社会现状，才是他的用意。

认为孟煌从此决定通过描述，来接近他必须面对的现实，无疑是错误的；同样，我们也不能断言柏林的生活给他的作品或思维带来了某种断层或怪异的转变。仅从他没有采用西方香烟的包装进行陈述这一点我们就能看出，他无意对现实世界中的美丽表象进行无谓的复制。烟盒的颜色是鲜艳的红色，这是一种在中国代表幸运和财富的色彩，它衬托出烟盒上用金色勾勒出来的天安门。一切是如此的照相写实，连上面的汉字和图案都一清二楚。这里，对细节的热衷和围绕精密刻划展开的游戏尽管显而易见，却没有对描绘对象的盲目崇拜，因为那个被捏得皱巴巴的烟盒不会让人觉得画家想要呈现的是美或者烟盒的设计，我们对它的阐释也就不能简化到有关纯粹审美效应的讨论上去。另外，孟煌还把这个变了形的烟盒置于一种云雾状、让人联想起烟的灰色背景之中，他甚至将这个红色烟盒和那些烟头画组合起来，以致我们不由地会去想象有一个人是如何一根接一根地抽完了最后一支烟。从打开烟盒，到抽完整盒香烟的那段时间对观看者来说，也就变得易于领会了。

尽管如此，以上这一重要提示也还未能让我们进入问题真正的关键所在。孟煌对"中华"这个烟名的影射在这里相当重要。中华烟在中国是一种在价格上让普通人无法承受的香烟，抽这种烟的人多是为了炫耀自己在商场的成功或官场的地位，表明自己进入了成功者或权力者的圈子。中华烟不仅是昂贵的身份象征，也是政治权力的符号，它常被用来送礼；在中国，烟是社会与经济交往的润滑油。那么，如果我们多关注一下这个烟名的文字意义，便能更加接近孟煌通过这种观念性图像组合想要表达的东西，翻译"中华"，能够让我们进入一个象征层面。你会突然明白它在某种程度上象征了"大中华"，明白孟煌之所以关注时间的流逝，也是意在指明万物——中国数千年的文化也不例外——无法逃避永久的轮回与最终的消亡，明白没有任何曾经的东西会永远如此下去。把空烟盒扔进垃圾桶前把它揉皱这最后一个动作，表达了画家对传统的批判态度。在他眼中，这种无休止重复着自己的传统不具有什么永远的重要性，而且早已过时。在与本文作者进行首次对话时，孟煌质疑了"中国人的行为和伦理规范"，认为它们"太过拘束于传统中国文化的影响"："我们的历史不去试图改变这一状况，却总是一再衍生出新的变体。尽管我们像西方人一样说话，穿衣品味差不多，甚至评断事物的标准也与西方人一样，但是在中国人这里，传统的世界观总有一席之地。我想通过我的作品表达的，是超越这一传统的重要性。"那么，那种日常生活中看似让一切变了模样的商业化，对孟煌来

factory would appear, smoke rising out of it, and then for a crucial moment he would sense true emotion. Looking at that distant scene, he had an unforgettable feeling, as if a meteorite had slammed straight into his heart. Even stronger, he had the almost physical sensation that a nail had been driven into his heart. Ever since then, for Meng Huang, the smokestack has been a powerful symbol of the despair of the individual spirit, which repeatedly inspires him to create paintings.

Based on this visual world, as well as on other landscapes in which colors are noticeably absent, the depiction of a crumpled *Cigarette Box* (2011, oil on canvas, 335 x 420 cm; 5x 335 x 84 cm) seems at first to be a surprising annoyance. Instead of just showing us the pack—which he obviously endows with great meaning, as evidenced by his selection of a large format for the image—he links it to a small-format series made up of twenty paintings (*Cigarettes No. 1*, 2011 – *Cigarettes No. 20*, 2011, oil on canvas, each 80 x 80 cm). These are of crushed cigarette butts in black ashtrays. Just one in the first picture, then two, then three, and at the end of the series, twenty. The number of images of cigarette butts corresponds to the number of cigarettes in a pack. Why? As people from the West, we involuntarily tend to make rapid comparisons and ask: why is the artist suddenly interested in the aesthetics of things that are rather trivial? Has he suddenly lost faith in himself? Will he, from now on, only cultivate the happiness and ease of pure self-abandon? Has he gone on a superficial trip and wandered by mistake into the waters of Pop Art? Is he familiar with the works of the French Nouveaux Réalistes? Or was his gaze simply captured by the commodified glamour of the packaging? However, these kinds of art historical conjectures are not really helpful here. They tend to distract us from what it is really all about, luring us onto the wrong track, instead of taking us behind the scenes of the first impression. Instead of getting lost among art historical citations, the actual task is to perceive the reality one experiences under social conditions that beset, oppress, and threaten the lives of individuals.

To accuse the artist of a simple descriptive approach to the reality he feels exposed to would be as wrong as it would be to assume that his sojourn in Berlin caused an abrupt break in his work or in his thoughts, or brought about a curious sort of turning point. Alone the fact that he does not use packs of western cigarettes suggests that this is something completely different from a simple, inconsequential copy of reality's beautiful façade. From out of the red of the cigarette pack—a color that symbolizes wealth and happiness in China—the image of Beijing's Temple of Heaven rises up. Here, everything is so photo-realistic that even individual words and symbols are legible. The pleasure in detail is remarkable, but is certainly not a sign of the painter's blind appreciation of the image depicted, because the cigarette pack is so crumpled that one can hardly come away with the impression that this is merely about the beauty or the design of a cigarette box. Consequently, the interpretation cannot be reduced to the simple statement that the painting is a revelation of pure aesthetics. Also, Meng Huang renders the deformed red package as if it were floating in front of a gray, foggy background that resembles clouds of smoke. Additionally, he combines the image with the other pictures of cigarette butts, so that we cannot help but imagine someone chain-smoking one cigarette after another. This also allows us, incidentally, to envision the time that passes from the point the pack is opened to when it is finally empty.

Yet, even this important reference does not penetrate to the actual core around which everything revolves. The question behind the significance of the cigarette brand Meng Huang alludes to is of considerable relevance. "Zhong Hua" is too expensive for the ordinary Chinese citizen; the brand is usually smoked by people who want to show that they have made something out of themselves in business, that they belong to the successful, the social climbers, or to those who have power in government. The brand has not only become an overpriced status symbol, but it also signifies political power, and is often given as a gift in order to further one's relationships and friendships. After all, in the People's Republic, cigarettes are considered the oil that greases the social and economic machines. We can come closer to what Meng Huang wants to express through this conceptual method of linking images, if we pay more attention to the brand name. Assisted by a translation of the phrase "Zhong Hua", we arrive at a symbolic level. Suddenly it becomes clear that the brand symbolizes the greatness of China, and that Meng Huang, with his perspective of temporality and the river of time, is also referring to eternal change and the end that comes to everyone and everything, without exception, even the People's Republic and its centuries-old culture—and that nothing can remain the same forever, or be what it once used to be. Crushing the cigarette package as a last act just before disposing of the rubbish

说，不是什么可以接受的选择，也不是什么真正意义上的改变，而是一种换汤不换药。取得这种关联却还是不能让我们结束对《烟》这件系列作品的阐释。它对社会现状的批判、它的象征性所具有的爆炸力，最后显现于 —— "抽"烟的"抽"字。"抽"也是"抽耳光"的"抽"。那么，那些被"抽"了的烟，便是被"抽"了耳光的权力。这件作品除了它的象征意义，还具有强烈的观念性，这体现于其中20幅小画加起来恰恰就是大画的面积，就像一盒烟有20根，20张画在这里填满了一幅大画。在这貌似无关痛痒的外衣之下，显然藏着一根极端否定的刺。

让我们从这里继续讨论《笼子》这件作品（2011，钢，3版，180 x 100 x 80 cm）。乍看，呈现于我们面前的似乎是一件普通的钢制抽象栅栏雕塑，然而，作品的结构却异常复杂。我们看到的，是一个有着中国国家地图轮廓的好像是空的笼子。孟煌无疑也是在通过它影射朋友艾未未的作品《中国地图》，他同时又添加了一个维度，进行了多个意义转化。首先，他用钢做的栅栏替代了艾未未作品中的木头。此举不仅暗喻了势态不断变化之中的"艾未未事件"，也隐喻了具有独立批判精神的（中国）知识分子的艰难处境与困境。这件作品不仅让我们联想到一个做成了等人高的狗笼子，它也在逼迫我们对人的生活与狗的生活进行类比，让我们联想到等着关押那些"找麻烦"的人的牢笼。这里，中国被整个地围了起来，成了一个笼子，而笼子意味着限制，和没有自由——总之，这是一个跟狗一般的人的生活的比喻。

2009年，孟煌开始创作系列摄影作品《走》（2009–2012，7版，16张黑白摄影系列作品，各75 x 62.5 cm），直至今日。《走》与他自己有关，也与对主观性"时间"的思考有关。我们在照片中看到的，是一个男子的肖像，不但他的发型和胡子在变，甚至他也在变得极其陌生。他有时披着披头士的长发，有时像个朋克，有时像个塔利班分子，有时又像个中国的知识分子，而发型也在跟着变。头发越长，胡子就越短；头发短了，他又把胡子蓄长；最后，胡子、头发、眉毛都被剪掉。从开始时的长头发、没胡子，到结束时被剃得精光的脑袋，毛发的生长和发型的改变不仅让我们看到时间在慢慢消逝。时间也在让照片里的人不再是从前的那个，他不断地变，最后变成了一个失去"本质"的存在。"京巴"这种半严肃半幽默的标题或许在向我们作着更为具体的暗示。它读上去像是一种存在主义式的表达，同时指向"我"的个人存在和"我"的身份。当一个中国人来到异域，面对陌生的文化，当"我"的文化像件行李被抛在身后的时候，会发生些什么呢？这种突然的文化转变会有什么影响呢？孟煌其实是在让自己这个初来乍到的中国人在西方的经验如浮云流水般地飘过。他在此间的个人表现却也有着某种普遍性，作品中用来伪装自己的突然的外表变化，象征了他在异域文化中的展开。在他亲身经历的同化过程的结尾处，我们看到的不是与"他"者百分之百的融合，而是绝对的"零"身份。在孟煌看来，"零"是一切可能状态中最好的状态。他的这些图像式思考带着古怪的幽默，带着些自我审视、自我嘲讽、甚至戏剧化的味道。这无疑源自于艺术家的生活经验，他懂得如何将这些个人经验游戏般地颠覆成某种具有普遍意义的东西。我们下面还会看到，他又重新拾起了"旅行"这个主题，并赋予它完全不同的内涵，以一种完全不同的方式提出"时间之本质"这一哲学命题。

《我 No. 2》（2004–2005，c-print，含52张宝丽莱照片扫描，56 x 167 cm）是一组让人颇为费神的一次成像摄影作品，创作始于2004年。它记录的不仅是艺术家在北京与河南之间一次带着政治与个人色彩的旅行，同时也是在探讨一件"原物"在几经沧桑之后还能留下什么。第一张是简简单单的自拍像，拍摄地点在河南他度过童年的地方。孟煌更希望以自己小时候的房子为背景，并从那里开始他的寻根之旅，只是，那座老楼早已夷为平地，也成为了"消亡"的象征。接下来的照片呈现的是艺术

embodies the artist's critical attitude toward endlessly perpetuated tradition, which is not eternally relevant and has been long outmoded, as far he is concerned. In his initial conversation with this author, he expressed skepticism toward "the behavior of people and the moral maxims in China," which, in his opinion, are "too strongly affected by traditional Chinese culture." "Instead of changing, our history continually repeats itself, over and over. Of course, we talk like people in the West. We also dress like them. Yes, even criteria are the same as in the West. But the old world view is still in effect. In my work I want to say that it is time to transcend the boundaries of this tradition." Consequently, the commercialization of everyday life, which tries to make everything appear in a new light, is neither an acceptable alternative for Meng Huang, nor a real change of any sort. Rather, it is merely a new means of continuing to perpetuate the old. Yet, even taking this into consideration, we have still not arrived at the end of our interpretation. We do not see all of the explosives hidden behind the symbolic critique of social conditions found in this series, until we learn that the Chinese word for "smoking" also means "a slap in the face". Hence, the cigarettes that are smoked represent a slap in the face to the powers that be. Aside from its symbolic charge, we see more of the conceptual plan behind the work when we realize that, as a group, the small paintings produce the same format as the large tableau. Just as the twenty cigarettes form the contents of the pack, the twenty paintings together fill up the space of the large one. Obviously, beneath this seemingly harmless surface lurks the sting of radical negation.

A work such as *Cage* (2011, steel, edition of 3, 180 x 100 x 80 cm) can also be accessed from this point, too. What at first seems like a completely normal sculpture made of steel bars turns out to be a considerably more complex construct. In front of us is an apparently empty cage in the basic geographical shape of China. By using the basic outline of the People's Republic, Meng Huang is clearly referring to the work *Map of China* by Ai Weiwei. Yet, he also lends it another dimension, and does more in the process than simply shift meaning. His use of steel bars instead of wood brings into play diverse allusions to the recurring problematic case of Ai Weiwei, as well as to the difficult circumstances and paradoxical situations critical intellectuals find themselves in. We are not only reminded of a human-size dog crate, forcing us to think of the analogy between a man's life and a dog's life, but we must also recall that prison awaits dissenters, those who march to a different drummer. All of China is barred, and consequently, is simply one big cage that sets boundaries and signifies bondage. All in all, we are dealing here with a metaphor for the human life that has gone to the dogs.

In *Go* (2009 – 2012, edition of 7, series of 16 b/w photographs, 16x 75 x 62.5 cm), a photo series encompassing the period from 2009 to the present, the artist not only deals with himself, but with the question of subjective time as well. We see the obscure self-portrait of a man whose changing hairdos and beards not only make him look different all of the time, but also strange. Sometimes he looks like a Beatle, with long hair. Sometimes like a punk. Sometimes like a member of the Taliban. Sometimes like a Chinese intellectual. And furthermore, there are coiffures that make him look very curious indeed. The longer the hair, the more clean-shaven he is; and the shorter the hair on his head, the wilder the beard is. Ultimately, at the end of the process, he has neither beard nor hair, nor eyebrows. The series begins with long hair and no beard, and it winds up with a completely bald head. Hair growth and changing hairstyles do more than just allow us to witness the passage of time, moment by moment. As time goes by, the man himself is no longer the person he once was; instead, he is always a different one, and in the end, he is a being without a nature. We can best see what he is specifically alluding to here if we read the semi-serious, semi-humorous title, *Go* (No. 1 – Pekingese), as if it were an existential statement about his own existence, as well as his own identity. What happens when a Chinese person finds himself abroad, subject to another culture, having left his own behind him, as if it were a piece of luggage? What are the consequences of this abrupt cultural exchange? Here, Meng Huang basically reviews his experience as a new Chinese arrival in the West. Yet, the sense of individuality he expresses here also contains a broad gesture. Seen in this way, the external changes—meaning the mutations his external appearance undergoes, which he presents in his series of photos as a process of disguising himself—are nothing but the signs of a long process of dissolving into another culture. However, the assimilation process does not end in total assimilation, but in an absolute lack of any identity whatsoever. From Meng Huang's point of view, this neutral state is the best of all possibilities, as he says. Buoyed by a rare sense of humor that has something self-questioning, self-ironic, even theatrical about it, these visual reflections can obviously be traced back to his own life experiences, which the artist knows how to playfully invert, generally speaking.

家旅途中的一些片刻，都是他随着自己的感受、情绪和直觉记录下来的各种地方、地点、题材、景致和场面。每次，孟煌都会把之前拍的那张宝丽莱照片摆在里面，也就是说，我们这里是在跟"像中像"打交道。我们看到他偶遇的路人、河南登封的永泰寺、中南海对面一家民警碰头的早餐店、颐和园里一个穿戏装为他唱歌的漂亮姑娘（他说，可惜她后来不见了）、在跳蚤市场淘到的革命书籍、2005年早春时他看到的第一朵花，还有北京北郊的一条臭水沟。然后，是他去看艾未未时艾未未正在创作的一件作品、一个在教女人跳舞、疯疯癫癫的老花花公子，以及黄河边的一座坟墓。

总而言之，都是寻根之旅中一些不相关联、随着时间渐渐淡去的标记。照片上留下的，不光是一些对孟煌有意义或追忆似水年华时迎面而来的景致，每张照片里都有另外一张改变了的、却有着之前所有照片里所有东西的宝丽莱照片。只是拍得越多，之前的东西在照片里就变得越小，最早的那张自拍像最后也还留在照片里，尽管并没有完全消失，却已小得无法分辨。本始之物最后留下了的，是几乎无从还原的一丝痕迹。此次个人经验对于孟煌，无非是他借以进行个性与共性表述的一个类比法，他真正关心的命题，是时间会让"本"或者"本源"怎样。我们同样可以把自我肖像的渐隐套用到马克思主义本源身上；后者也只剩下了一丝痕迹，并且还在继续消亡。数十年后的今天，人们与之渐行渐远，在那遥远地方的某一处，它还隐现着一丁点痕迹。孟煌在作品中表现出来的个人主义的背后，埋伏着一种基于自身体验、摆荡于个体与共性之间的历史观。关于"永久"的学说难道只是一种神话？—— 我们得这样发问。

Now, we will see how he once again deals with the motif of the journey, while giving it an entirely different set of contents, thus posing the philosophical question about the nature of time in a completely different way. *I No. 2* (2004–2005, edition of 7, c-print including 52 scanned Polaroid photos, 56 x 167 cm) is the title of one of the challenging Polaroid photo series with which he began the year 2004. It documents more than just his politically and personally motivated journey between Henan and Beijing. At the same time, it explores the issue of what is left of an original after time and tides have passed. At the very start, the series begins with a self-portrait taken in Henan, the province in which he spent his childhood. He would have preferred to use the house where he grew up as the starting point for his return journey to his roots, but it was demolished long ago and thus now symbolizes extinction. For other photos portraying the course of his journey, moment by moment, he selected places along the way—very different sites, towns, motifs, and scenes—in accordance with his feelings, mood, and intuition. To these he added each Polaroid photo he had taken before. To put it another way, we are dealing with pictures within pictures here. We see, for instance, people he just happened to run into. The Yong Tai Temple in Deng Feng. A breakfast place across from Zhong Nan Hai, where plainclothes policemen meet. A beautiful girl in an opera costume, who sang for him in the Summer Palace, although he unfortunately lost sight of her later, as he notes in conversation. As well as books on the revolution, discovered at a flea market. Or the first flower he saw in spring 2005. An above-ground sewer ditch in a suburb north of Beijing. Then a work of art that Ai Wei-wei happened to be laboring over when he visited him... A crazy old playboy who gave dancing lessons to women. When Meng Huang asked him for a favor, the old man turned his back on him. And he also took a photo of a gravesite along the Yellow River.

All in all, casual signs marking a journey to his roots, which fade more and more as time goes by. The photos not only capture the motifs that have some meaning to him, or jumped out at him while he was on his search for lost time—each one also contains an altered Polaroid photo, entailing everything he photographed before along the way. Yet, the more often he repeated the process of adding a Polaroid to a new picture, the smaller the things in the older pictures became. In the end the self-portrait from the beginning is still there, somewhere, but because it has become smaller and smaller, it has also become increasingly difficult to recognize—although it has not disappeared entirely. Ultimately, the only thing left of the original is a touch of a vague trace, almost impossible to reconstruct. For Meng Huang this personal experience is just an analogy that he uses to try to formulate something that is simultaneously specific and general, because the question that ultimately motivates him has to do with what happens to the source or the original over time. The gradual disappearance of the self-portrait might also allude to the original idea of Marxism, because, at the most, only a gradually vanishing trace of it is left, too. Over the decades, man has gotten further and further away from it. Somewhere in the distance a tiny little bit of it can still be seen. Behind the things that Meng Huang individualizes in his work lurks a theory of history based on his own experiences, which oscillates between the individual and the global. Is the theory of perpetuity nothing more than a fiction? It is a question that must be asked.

Translated from German: Allison Plath-Moseley

展览作品 Exhibited Works

《走》2009－2012, 7版
16张黑白摄影作品系列
每一张约 75 x 62.5 cm

"Go" 2009－2012, edition of 7
series of 16 b/w photographs
16x 75 x 62.5 cm

《走》2009－2012, 局部　　　"Go" 2009－2012, detail
(No. 02－爆炸)　　　　　　　(No. 02－Explosion)

《走》2009 – 2012, 局部   "Go" 2009 – 2012, detail
（No. 04 – 牛王）   (No. 04 – Lucifer)

《走》2009 - 2012, 局部   "Go" 2009 - 2012, detail
(No. 12 - 达摩)   (No. 12 - Dharma)

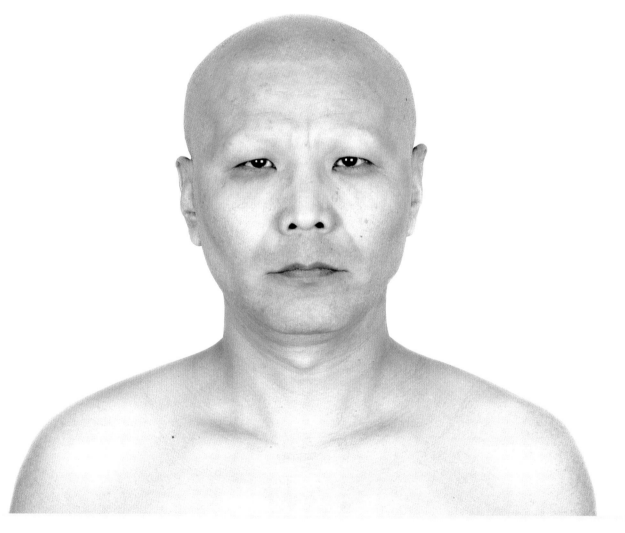

《走》2009‒2012, 局部
(No. 16‒大同)

"Go" 2009‒2012, detail
(No. 16‒Great Harmony)

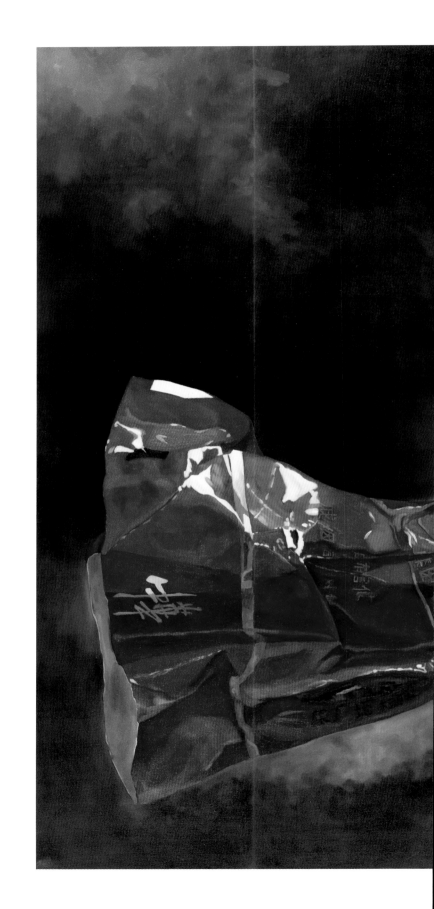

《烟盒》2011
布面油画
335 x 420 cm (5x 335 x 84 cm)

"Cigarette Box" 2011
oil on canvas
335 x 420 cm (5x 335 x 84 cm)

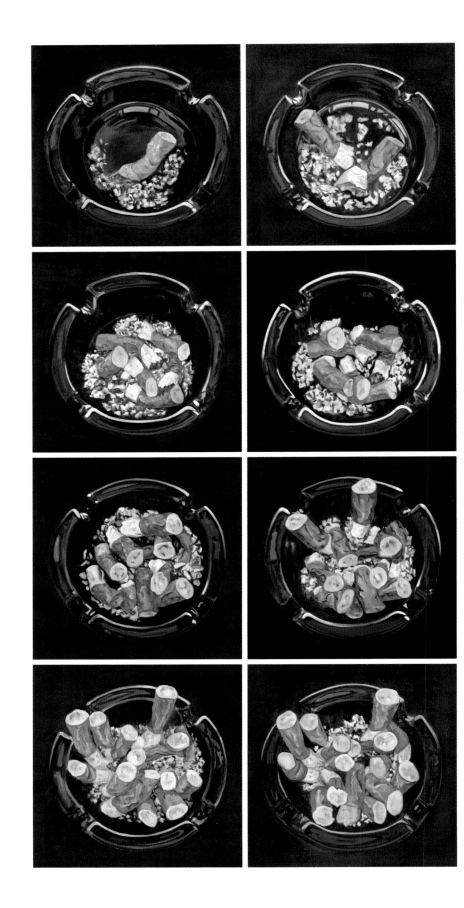

《香烟 No. 1》2011 –《香烟 No. 20》2011
布面油画
每幅 80 x 80 cm

"Cigarettes No. 1" 2011 – "Cigarettes No. 20" 2011
oil on canvas
each 80 x 80 cm

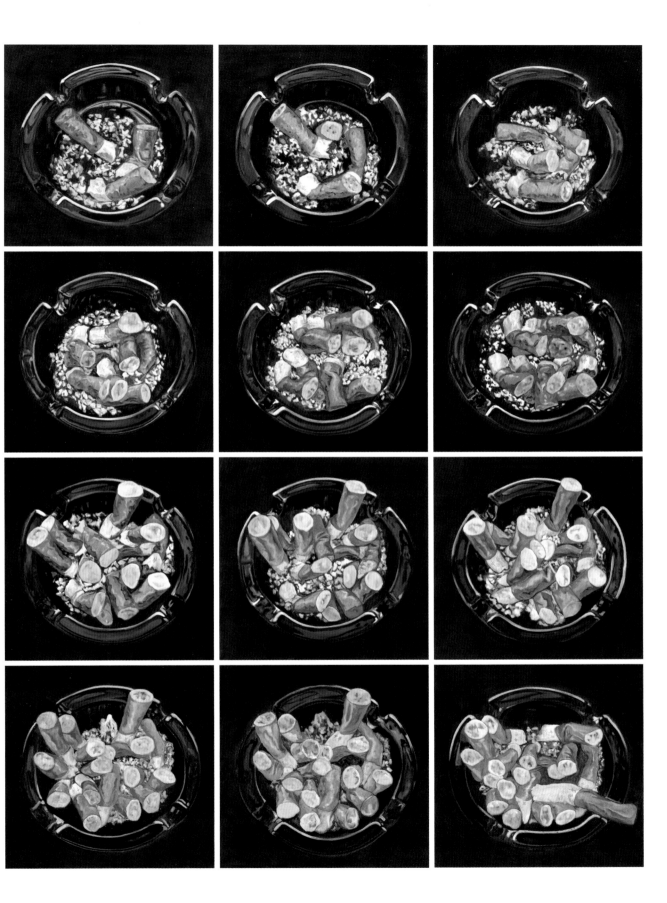

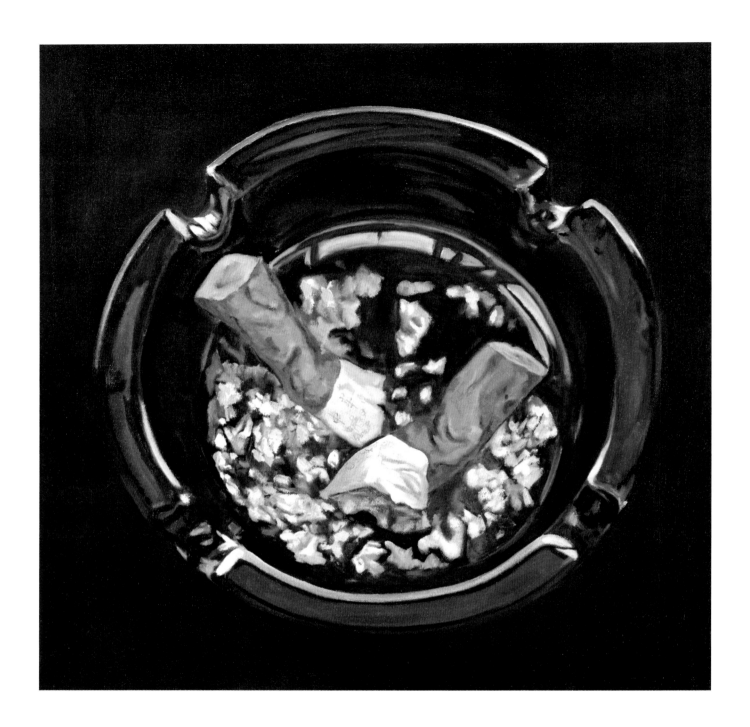

《香烟 No. 2》2011   "Cigarettes No. 2" 2011
布面油画   oil on canvas
80 x 80 cm   80 x 80 cm

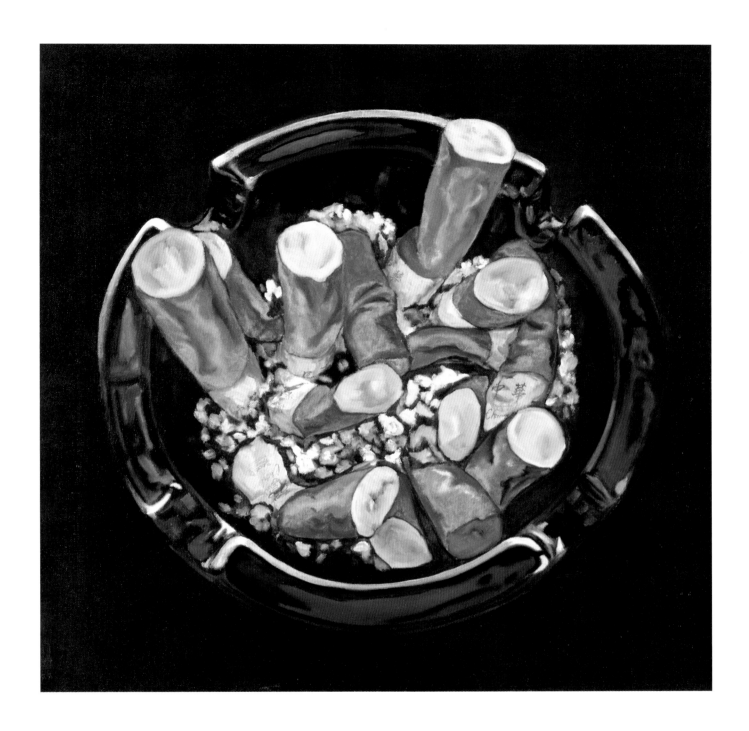

《香烟 No. 14》2011   "Cigarettes No. 14" 2011
布面油画   oil on canvas
80 x 80 cm   80 x 80 cm

《我 No. 2》2004–2005, 7版
c-print 包含52张宝丽莱照片
56 x 167 cm

"I No. 2" 2004–2005, edition of 7
c-print including 52 scanned Polaroid photos
56 x 167 cm

《我 No. 2》2004-2005, 8张局部　　"I No. 2" 2004-2005, 8 details

《笼子》2011, 3版
钢
180 x 100 x 80 cm

"Cage" 2011, edition of 3
steel
180 x 100 x 80 cm

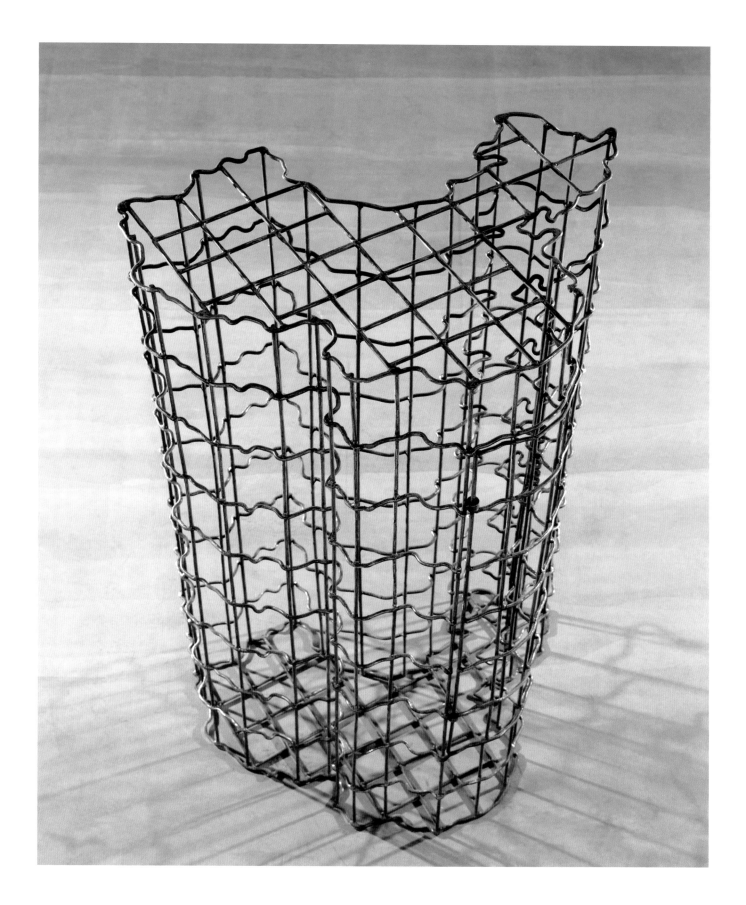

《笼子》2011, 局部　　"Cage" 2011, detail

孟煌 "我和我们" 展览现场, 麦勒画廊 北京-卢森, 瑞士卢森, 2012
Exhibition view, Meng Huang "I and We", Galerie Urs Meile, Beijing-Lucerne, Lucerne, Switzerland, 2012

孟煌 "我和我们" 展览现场, 麦勒画廊 北京-卢森, 瑞士卢森, 2012
Exhibition view, Meng Huang "I and We", Galerie Urs Meile, Beijing-Lucerne, Lucerne, Switzerland, 2012

其它近期作品 Other Recent Works

《我们的天空之传统篇》2011
布面油画
400 x 220 cm

"Our Sky – Traditional Phase" 2011
oil on canvas
400 x 220 cm

《我们的天空之改革篇》2011   "Our Sky – Revolutionary Phase" 2011
布面油画   oil on canvas
400 x 220 cm   400 x 220 cm

《远方 No. 1》2011　　　"Distance No. 1" 2011
布面油画　　　　　　　oil on canvas
180 x 280 cm　　　　　180 x 280 cm

《远方 No. 2》2011   "Distance No. 2" 2011
布面油画   oil on canvas
180 x 280 cm   180 x 280 cm

《椅子 No. 1》–《椅子 No. 5》, 2011

文：萧岭

椅子系列 (《椅子No. 1》–《椅子No. 5》, 2011) 的这组作品包括五张黑白油画, 每张作品都从一个不同的角度描绘了一把空椅子, 影射出人们对待同一个话题也会持有截然不同的见解。就像孟煌的其他作品一样, 他选择的主题总是充满着艺术史与政治话题的多重指向以及丰富的象征涵义。这组系列作品中看似平凡普通的木制椅子不由让人联想到梵高 (Van Gogh) 曾经描画过的空椅子, 这也暗指这位艺术大师的才华在其有生之年不被认可。如果椅子可以被看作是政治权力的象征, 那么孟煌所刻画的椅子不仅隐喻着包括刘晓波在内的中国异见知识分子在拘留期间每天都会坐的椅子, 还用空椅子的形象暗指了在2010年诺贝尔和平奖颁奖仪式上, 获奖者刘晓波的缺席。椅子系列还与艺术家于2011年在柏林做过的一个行为作品有关。为了表示对朋友刘晓波的支持, 孟煌在跳蚤市场买了一把椅子并扛着它穿过了柏林的大街小巷, 最后抵达一个邮局。在那里, 孟煌将椅子包装好, 寄到了刘晓波正在被拘留的处所 —— 辽宁省锦州监狱。而艺术家在绘画作品中所描绘的, 正是这把椅子。

Chair No. 1 – Chair No. 5, 2011

by Nataline Colonnello

The Chair series (*Chair No. 1* through *Chair No. 5*, all 2011) is comprised of five black and white paintings, each portraying a chair seen from a different perspective, metaphorically suggesting the dissimilar viewpoints people might have on the same topic. As is the case for many of Meng Huang's works, his chosen subject is imbued with highly symbolic and multi-layered references to both art history and politics. The ordinary, straw-bottomed wooden chair that Meng Huang selected for this series is reminiscent of those empty ones depicted by Van Gogh, hinting at the fact that the master painter's talent went unrecognized while he was alive. If a chair can be seen as an emblem of political power, Meng Huang's represents not only that on which a dissident intellectual such as Liu Xiaobo might sit everyday during years of detention in his own country, but also the vacant seat the very same dissident left empty during a celebratory ceremony that he could never have attended, where he was honored with the Nobel Peace Prize in 2010. The Chair series is related to a performance Meng Huang held in Berlin in March 2011 in token of support for his friend Liu Xiaobo. In the performance, Meng Huang bought the chair later represented in the five canvasses at the flea market and carried it through the streets until he reached the post office, where it was packed and eventually posted to Liu Xiaobo at his address in Jinzhou Prison in Liaoning Province, China.

《椅子 No. 1》2011　　"Chair No. 1" 2011
布面油画　　　　　 oil on canvas
100 x 80 cm　　　　 100 x 80 cm

《椅子 No. 2》2011   "Chair No. 2" 2011
布面油画   oil on canvas
100 x 80 cm   100 x 80 cm

《椅子 No. 3》2011   "Chair No. 3" 2011
布面油画   oil on canvas
100 x 80 cm   100 x 80 cm

《椅子 No. 4》2011   "Chair No. 4" 2011   《椅子 No. 5》2011   "Chair No. 5" 2011
布面油画   oil on canvas   布面油画   oil on canvas
100 x 80 cm   100 x 80 cm   100 x 80 cm   100 x 80 cm

《早上好 No. 1》2010
布面油画
280 x 220 cm

"Guten Morgen No. 1" 2010
oil on canvas
280 x 220 cm

《早上好 No. 2》 2010
布面油画
280 x 220 cm

"Guten Morgen No. 2" 2010
oil on canvas
280 x 220 cm

《锈》2009, 局部　　"Rust" 2009, detail

《锈》2009, 3版
17个钢制汉字, 表面有弹孔痕迹
195 x 410 x 6 cm

"Rust" 2009, edition of 3
17 steel characters pierced by gun bullets
195 x 410 x 6 cm

这些是中国犯人刚进监狱时会被问到的三句话：

"你是谁？"
"这里是什么地方？"
"你到这里干什么？"

这些立体文字的背面留有子弹射击和枪眼的痕迹
（每个字约 55 x 60 x 7 cm）。

The writings represent the three sentences a prisoner can find as soon as he enters any jail in China:

"Who are you?"
"What place is this?"
"For which purpose did you come here?"

The letters are three-dimensional (each character ca. 55 x 60 x 7 cm) with damage and holes caused by bullet-shots to the back side.

孟煌

1966   生于中国北京
        生活和工作在中国北京与德国柏林

主要个展

2012   "我和我们", 麦勒画廊 北京-卢森, 瑞士卢森
2010   "人的五个面", WiE Kultur, 德国柏林
2009   "时间和地点——孟煌个展", 上海比翼艺术中心, 中国上海
2008   "你说呢? 风景", 麦勒画廊 北京-卢森, 中国北京
2006   "孟煌——水景", 麦勒画廊 北京-卢森, 瑞士卢森
        "风景", 力透空间, 中国北京
2000   "失乐园——孟煌个展", 艺术文件仓库 (CAAW), 中国北京

主要联展

2011   "Weltsichten. Landschaft in der Kunst seit dem 17. Jahrhundert", 威斯巴登博物馆, 德国威斯巴登
        "Weltsichten. Landschaft in der Kunst seit dem 17. Jahrhundert", 基尔艺术馆, 德国基尔
2010   "Cantieri Mutanti", 原精神病医院厨房, 意大利Pergine Valsugana
        "Weltsichten. Landschaft in der Kunst seit dem 17. Jahrhundert", Situation Kunst, 德国波鸿
2009   "态度", 泄特艺术中心, 中国郑州
2008   "中国艺术家与欧盟主席若泽·曼努埃尔·巴罗佐先生的对话——奥运会后中国北京的文化景观专题展", 欧共体中国代表团,
        欧盟驻北京大使馆, 中国北京
        "一间房, 两星期, 二十三位艺术家", 拉合尔美术协会 (Alhamra), 巴基斯坦拉合尔
2006   "麻将——希克中国现代艺术收藏展", 汉堡艺术馆, 德国汉堡
2005   "中国: 当代艺术的方向", Oberdan空间, 意大利米兰
        "形象的基因: 中国制造", 麦勒画廊 北京-卢森, 瑞士卢森
        "麻将——希克收藏中国现代艺术品展", 伯尔尼美术馆, 瑞士伯尔尼
        "翻手为云, 覆手为雨", TS1 (宋庄一号) 当代艺术中心, 中国北京
2003   "七件作品", 艺术文件仓库 (CAAW), 中国北京
        "交融——中国、韩国、马来西亚、新加坡9位艺术家作品展", 季节画廊, 中国北京
        "风景", 犀锐艺术中心, 中国北京
2001   艺术文件仓库 (CAAW) 开幕展, 中国北京
        "真实可能", 中央美院画廊, 中国北京
        "新配方", 东大名创库, 中国上海
        艺术家仓库开幕展, 艺术家仓库, 中国北京
        "相聚德胜门", 德胜门, 中国北京
        第一届成都双年展, 成都现代艺术馆, 中国成都
2000   "主题·媒介·意义——各就各位", 中央美院画廊, 中国北京
        "不合作方式", 上海东廊, 中国上海
1999   "观念, 色彩和感性", 艺术文件仓库 (CAAW), 中国北京

Meng Huang

1966   born in Beijing, China
        lives and works in Beijing, China and Berlin, Germany

Selected Solo Exhibitions

2012   "I and We", Galerie Urs Meile, Beijing-Lucerne, Lucerne, Switzerland

2010   "Five Faces of a Man", WiE Kultur, Berlin, Germany

2009   "Time and Place – Meng Huang's Solo Exhibition", BizArt Art Center, Shanghai, China

2008   "And What Do You Think? Landscapes", Galerie Urs Meile, Beijing-Lucerne, Beijing, China

2006   "Meng Huang – Waterscapes", Galerie Urs Meile, Beijing-Lucerne, Lucerne, Switzerland

        "Windscape", Litou Space, Beijing, China

2000   "Lost Paradise – Meng Huang's Solo Exhibition", China Art Archives & Warehouse (CAAW), Beijing, China

Selected Group Exhibitions

2011   "Weltsichten. Landschaft in der Kunst seit dem 17. Jahrhundert", Museum Wiesbaden, Wiesbaden, Germany

        "Weltsichten. Landschaft in der Kunst seit dem 17. Jahrhundert", Kunsthalle zu Kiel, Kiel, Germany

2010   "Cantieri Mutanti", Cucine ex Ospedale Psichiatrico, Pergine Valsugana, Italy

        "Weltsichten. Landschaft in der Kunst seit dem 17. Jahrhundert", Situation Kunst, Bochum, Germany

2009   "Attitude", Shit-Art Center, Zhengzhou, China

2008   Special Exhibition in association with "Dialogue between Chinese artists and the President of the European Commission, Mr. José Manuel Barroso, on the cultural landscape in China-Beijing, after the Olympic Games", Delegation of the European Commission to China, Beijing, China

        "1 House, 2 Weeks, 23 Artists", The Lahore Arts Council (Alhamra), Lahore, Pakistan

2006   "Mahjong – Chinesische Gegenwartskunst aus der Sammlung Sigg", Hamburger Kunsthalle, Hamburg, Germany

2005   "China: As Seen by Contemporary Chinese Artists", Spazio Oberdan, Milan, Italy

        "Pictorial DNA Made in China", Galerie Urs Meile, Beijing-Lucerne, Lucerne, Switzerland

        "Mahjong – Chinesische Gegenwartskunst aus der Sammlung Sigg", Kunstmuseum Bern, Berne, Switzerland

        "Conspire", TS1 Contemporary Art Centre, Beijing, China

2003   "7 Works", China Art Archives & Warehouse (CAAW), Beijing, China

        "Interfusion – 9 Leading Artists from China, Korea, Malaysia, Singapore", Art Seasons Gallery, Beijing, China

        "Landscapes", X-Ray Art Centre, Beijing, China

2001   Inauguration Exhibition of the New Gallery, China Art Archives & Warehouse (CAAW), Beijing, China

        "Reality Possibility", The Art Gallery of the Central Academy of Fine Arts, Beijing, China

        "New Prescription", Dongdaming Creative Space, Shanghai, China

        Inauguration of Artists Warehouse, Artists Warehouse, Beijing, China

        "Being Together at Deshengmen", Deshengmen, Beijing, China

        1st Chengdu Biennial, Chengdu Museum of Modern Art, Chengdu, China

2000   "Subject-Media-Meaning - Everyone His Own Position", The Art Gallery of the Central Academy of Fine Arts, Beijing, China

        "Fuck Off", Eastlink Gallery, Shanghai, China

1999   "Concepts, Colors and Passions", China Art Archives & Warehouse (CAAW), Beijing, China

GALERIE URS MEILE
BEIJING · LUCERNE

麦 勒 画 廊
北 京 · 卢 森

出版: 麦勒画廊 北京-卢森

编辑: 麦勒画廊 北京-卢森
文章: Heinz-Norbert Jocks
翻译: Allison Plath-Moseley (英)
设计: 李建辉
摄影: Patrick Bussmann, Nadine Ethner, 方余龙, Ali Ghandtschi, Eric Gregory Powell

印刷: 中国北京

Publisher: Galerie Urs Meile, Beijing-Lucerne

Editor: Galerie Urs Meile, Beijing-Lucerne
Text: Heinz-Norbert Jocks
Translator: Allison Plath-Moseley (E)
Designer: Li Jianhui
Photography: Patrick Bussmann, Nadine Ethner, Fang Yulong, Ali Ghandtschi, Eric Gregory Powell

ISBN: 978-3-9523767-6-8

Printed in China

麦勒画廊, 北京市朝阳区草场地104号, 邮编 100015, 电话 +86 10 643 333 93
Galerie Urs Meile, No. 104, Caochangdi, Chaoyang District, Beijing, PRC 100015, T +86 10 643 333 93
Galerie Urs Meile, Rosenberghöhe 4, 6004 Lucerne, Switzerland, T +41 41 420 33 18
galerie@galerieursmeile.com, www.galerieursmeile.com